Is Your Life Out of Order?

By D. L. Crager
&
Shelly Crager

Illustrated by Crystal Myers

Trilogy Christian Publishers
A Wholly Owned Subsidiary of Trinity Broadcasting Network
2442 Michelle Drive
Tustin, CA 92780
Copyright © 2022 by D. L. and Shelly Crager
Illustrated by Crystal Myers

For information, address Trilogy Christian Publishing
Rights Department, 2442 Michelle Drive, Tustin, Ca 92780.
Trilogy Christian Publishing/ TBN and colophon are trademarks of Trinity Broadcasting Network.
For information about special discounts for bulk purchases, please contact Trilogy Christian Publishing.
Manufactured in the United States of America

Trilogy Disclaimer: The views and content expressed in this book are those of the author and may not necessarily reflect the views and doctrine of Trilogy Christian Publishing or the Trinity Broadcasting Network.

10 9 8 7 6 5 4 3 2 1
Library of Congress Cataloging-in-Publication Data is available.
ISBN: 978-1-63769-946-1
E-ISBN: 978-1-63769-947-8

Table of Contents

1 Is this Your Life 5

2 Where do You Fit In 15

3 The Secret 29

4 Who's Leading 47

5 Catapult Your Family 59

6 Give the Best Gift 67

7 Your Heart's Desire 79

8 Power Source 93

Chapter 1

Is this Your Life

Disappointing, dysfunctional, frustrating, painful, lonely, and void of balance, joy, and contentment. Are these words describing your life, marriage, career, and even your children? Are you struggling to get through the day without a headache or heartache? Or, are you simply seeking fresh knowledge and direction for purpose and organization in your daily life?

If you're *married*, are you continually arguing over hurdles or situations: sex, money, time, the past, personality differences, baggage, what the other is doing or not doing? Are the kids out of control and never listening or behaving?

Maybe you're *single or divorced* and life is empty and/or feels like you're trying to run across on a lake of ice, hoping you won't fall through, but are going nowhere fast, as you constantly slip and slide, and painfully fall here and there.

Are you tired all the time, dreading getting up in the morning or going to work? Overwhelmed there is so much to do and very little time, as *purpose* for everything has completely disappeared, and the point to life has lost its meaning? Where is your *heart*?

When was the last time your heart was full? You know what we're talking about, when enthusiasm, gratitude and peacefulness swelled within you so much, it easily permeated out of you, by your actions as well as your words and attitude. Are you searching for balance, joy and a content life that has *hope* again, which has been lost or forgotten somewhere down the road? Are you needing inspiration to have purpose to move forward and put your life back in order?

A. How would you describe your life right now?

If we are on the same page, let us give you a visual to help easily explain where your life might be right now. It has become exactly like a vending machine that's *out of order*. Look at the cover of this book. You're standing, looking into the vending machine (of your life), angry or disappointed. You see the packages of (life's) food that will satisfy your (life's) hunger. But you can't get anything because your (life's) machine is out of order.

We didn't say *broken*. We said, *out of order*. There is a big difference.

Now, you have the desire for these different foods of life, as well as the knowledge and ability to work your life's machine. But because the machine is *out of order*, you will not be fulfilled and will go away empty, frustrated, and disappointed with no hope in sight. Is this a mirror image of your life or marriage? Has life become so painful and energy-depleting, that it's surrounded by constant storms and has lost vision to the point where it is void of balance, joy, and contentment?

Why does this happen to a majority of individuals and marriages alike? How did it happen, and what are the root causes for having a life out of order? Is this new or has this been an ongoing issue, just with different people, places, and times?

B. What hurdles or situations do you believe are contributing to your life being out of order? Maybe it's who?

Our goal in writing this book is to *communicate* a powerful but simple tool for your life so you'll have the *awareness* to what is possibly wrong with your relationships, so you will be able to *adjust* or *solve* what is hindering or destroying them in order to start the *healing* process. Once you're on the healing path, your relationships will start to *strengthen* and you'll be on your way towards *progress* and *growth* for a balanced, joyful, and content life. All because you will have clarity of why it is so important to have your relationships in order, which will bring life-long hope from rejuvenating inspiration that leads to understanding life's ultimate purpose.

*

You, the reader, tell us, "But I don't want to heal or make progress in my messed-up life or marriage. I just want out!"

*

Oh, so you're just going to give up and be a statistic and flounder emotionally, psychologically, relationally, and spiritually? Even worse, you would possibly do this to your children's lives, giving them the excuse and example of how to give up and fail with relationships?

*

Your response, "How dare you! You have no idea of the awful things I've been through." *Or*, "I've been married to this person for so many years and have put up with so many things. I've tried to make it work, but they are who they are and they won't change. You don't know the pathetic excuse of a husband/wife I have and the pain they've put me through. I get nothing out of this marriage or them. Our children are monsters and are suffering because our family is so screwed up. There is *no* hope!"

*

You're right, we don't know the exact pain and suffering you've been through, or are going through, and you don't know what we've been through either. But in our lives, and in thirty plus years of marriage, our family is not without its own pains and struggles, which we will discuss in later chapters, as we have also listened to and witnessed in more couples and families than we can count.

But we will strongly interject from your *'no hope'* comment. In the moments of anguish, and in the constant escalation of hurdles and negative circumstances, many times it does appear that hope is erased, leaving us empty with no living compass for direction that only influences us to believe that life is pointless and is heading to a dead end.

Here's an analogy. When we're too close to a painting of a grand and beautiful landscape, and are only looking at one small corner, all we see is one small portion of the whole painting. From this perspective you have *no idea* what the whole and finished portrait is about.

While we're this close to the canvas (life's hurdles and situations), we begin to focus on the details of the brush strokes—perfect and imperfect alike—and only see the graphic textures (smooth, sharp, lumpy, etc.) of the dried paint that are only lines and splotches that have no rhyme or reason for their design or color (existence). Being this close to the painting, we cannot see the artist's story for taking the time to create the large masterpiece.

In this illustration we can begin to understand how our perspective, attitude, and knowledge can be severely skewed, leading us astray from life having any hope or purpose, when we are not wisely standing back and viewing the big picture of our lives.

C. Have you positioned yourself physically, mentally, or emotionally so close to life's circumstances and hurdles that you have lost focus of the big picture of your and/or your family's life? What and why?

We are going to split up into two different defining categories of what we consider *troubles* or *problems* in our lives to simplify our thinking and understanding.

    1. *Obstacles and Hurdles*

    2. *Situations and Circumstances*

Life's *obstacles and hurdles* are generally routine in most lives, marriages, and/or families.

- Only one spouse is truly trying to grow, to make it work, and get help

- Communication (lack thereof, or not speaking the others personality language)
- Money
- Sexual frustration
- Control issues
- Fear and worry
- Trust
- Forgiveness
- Unfaithfulness
- Time management
- Carrying past baggage (bad experiences, mental, emotional, physical, spiritual)
- Loneliness
- Addictions (alcohol, drugs, pornography, eating, social media, etc.)
- Compatibility (mismatched personalities, interests, spiritual beliefs)
- Abuse (physical, mental, emotional, spiritual)
- Physical/mental/psychological obstacles (O.C.D., A.D.D., P.T.S.D., bipolar disorder, depression, sleep deprivation, narcissism, mental/physical handicaps, etc.)
- Selfishness
- Life's priorities, specifically relationships, are completely *out of order*

We have named some possible *thorns* for individual, family, marital, and relational stress and destruction. Did we hit the nail on the head with you?

D. Which of these hurdles are a struggle in your marriage and/or family? Maybe you have multiple hurdles, which is common for many individuals and couples alike.

The other category, where there are other problems in our lives, is with *situations and circumstances*. They feel more like stepping on a porcupine or in a mud puddle, and generally come and go. They are repercussions of things that happen in life such as: getting sick, getting into a fight, a death in the family, losing a job, burning dinner, bankruptcy, child problems, car accident, a fire or flood in the house, missing a flight at the airport—this list goes on and on.

Like a sharp prick of a porcupine quill or the messy mud puddle, there are things in life that just happen, as many are unexpected. They sting and sometimes create a permanent stain, but at the same time, are forming and shaping the portrait of our lives through experience.

This book is not meant to help remove the porcupines or mud puddles in your life, but instead, to simply recognize they are there, and that they *can significantly and positively* shape you and the relationships in your life, even though they can be painful or messy. But only if you are wisely standing back and looking at your life's portrait as a whole, and not just one small area, along with the right attitude.

We are on an incredible journey, and have a spectacular, balanced, joyful, and content marriage, but not one without its own hurdles and circumstances, of course, which we will be sharing some of them later as well.

No matter if you're single, newlyweds, have been married for fifty plus years, or are on your second marriage, we want to share with you a *simple and powerful tool* that we have also shared and demonstrated with countless people over the years. It is a simple visual to understand and remember, that will help guide you on how to find balance, joy, and contentment, by prioritizing your relationships as you weave your way through a continuous, imperfect, dark world, filled with brokenness, and begin to *thrive* through the struggles that will always come your way.

Chapter 2

Where do You Fit In

To help you realize that *you're not alone*, and to begin uncovering the hurdles and situations in the different relationships of your life that may be out of order, we have staged three different life scenarios. As you read through them, identify the area(s) in which you would say, "Yes, that's me, or us!" Maybe it was your family growing up, or a mirror image of the family next door.

Scenario #1

'Everything and more...'

I'm doing everything around here, and I'm getting tired of it! Janice thought to herself as she put the last plate into the dishwasher and aggressively closed the door. She turned around and leaned her backside on the counter, then crossed her arms. It was late evening, and she was tired and frustrated—again. Janice's day was filled with a schedule of things to do that never ended; only repeating itself over and over every day.

She had already put the kids to bed, as Marv (her husband) was in his office behind the computer. Janice looked his direction from where she stood, and through the French doors, she could see him playing or working on something. At this moment she didn't care what he was doing.

Why should I care? she thought to herself. *He doesn't care about what I'm doing, or have done, or anything else, except for what he does on that stupid computer every night.*

She left the kitchen to go to the bedroom, walking past his office without looking in, and said in an irritated tone, "I'm going to bed."

"What?" Marv asked, keeping his eyes focused on the screen.

"Nothing," Janice responded, disgruntled, as she kept walking into their bedroom and through to the bathroom. Stopping at the sink, she looked up at the person in the mirror.

"Here we are again!" she stated sarcastically. Janice stood there at the end of another day, asking the woman looking back at her as she has so many times before, "Is this how life is supposed to be? Is this the great plan for marriage and raising kids? If it is, I hate it! I don't know if I want to continue on. How about you?" She starred at her reflection waiting for an answer.

Marv heard Janice walk by the office saying something, not clearly hearing what she said, and answered to himself, *No matter, she's always moody and constantly complaining about me, the kids, and everything else.* He raised his head and whispered aloud, "I wish she would show me some appreciation for all the hard work I do for my family. I bust my butt all day long so she can have all this." He looked up through the glass doors of the office into their home, then back down refocusing on where he was in the video game, and continued playing.

Inadvertently, Marv is hiding from the world that has become unsatisfying, tiring, chaotic, and without purpose. For a long time now, Marv has been trying to find satisfaction sitting by himself in a fantasy world. One that has simple order, no pain, and grand excitement that the real world doesn't seem to provide. If the game doesn't go his way or gets too hard, all he has to do is press the reset button to start over whenever he wants. Even though the game, or whatever he has on the computer screen, is all an illusion, it's an easy world to live in, unlike what his real life and family has become.

Janice and Marv have been married for thirteen years and have three children. They go to church and are involved in different ministries. Marv is a hard worker and is a good provider for his family. He puts in at least fifty hours a week with his job, many times bringing his work home to his own office. His primary focus in life is his career, always in pursuit of the next promotion and raise, which hopefully is soon because everything is getting expensive. The kids are growing and are always needing new clothes and toys, and then there's college to save for.

Right out of college, Janice had started a career, but after having their second child, she and Marv thought it best for her to be a stay-at-home mom, even though it seems she's never at home. However, when she is at home her daily tasks involve: doing a load or two of laundry, loading and unloading the dishwasher, dumping the trash, cleaning up after the kids and Marv all over the house, making four beds, taking care of the dog and cat, and having dinner ready at the end of the day. Not to mention doing all this and taking care of their one-year-old all day long as their other two children are at school.

When she leaves the house, she goes to multiple places, depending on the day of the week. The grocery store is an every other day stop, as well as other stores for household items and family things. She is part of the PTA at her kids' schools, which takes up part of a day during the week. Then she visits her mother three times a week, for an hour or two, making sure she's getting along with her physical disability while living alone. Last, but not least, don't forget the weekly women's Bible study and worship team practice to be ready for Sunday.

Marv puts in the time at work to be the good provider for his family, but not too much time that he misses out on the fun with the guys. A basketball game at the gym or a softball game once or twice a week depending on the season. Yes, they take up a lot of his evenings, but he'll tell you it's all for the sake of exercise. Then the weekend warrior comes out of him every time there's something to hunt or fish. Who knows what he's going to do this weekend.

Janice gets up early every morning before her family and goes to the gym to workout. She is very conscious about how healthy she is, but truthfully, how she looks is much more important. She gets her hair and nails done every week, as well as making sure her year-round tan stays the same color.

Their kids, who are one, eight, and eleven years old, keep them busy with school things: programs, teacher conferences, and open houses for each grade. Then their activities out of school: gymnastic practices and meets, baseball and football practices and games, all going on at the same time, which now seems to endlessly go on throughout the year.

Homework, dinner, the kids playing and fighting every evening, is an indoor hurricane physically and emotionally, with the storm repeating itself every night.

For Janice and Marv, finding alone time is always a challenge. When they do have intimate moments, it's not what it used to be, or what they want it to be. Janice is always tired, and very rarely is she in the mood. Most of the time, she's dreading it and can't wait to get it over with, as Marv gets frustrated because she's not the wild woman she used to be in bed, or fantasizes her to be.

So many nights, they end up barely saying a word to one another, and just roll away from the other, falling asleep; only to wake up to another day of the same, tiring, chaotic, and purposeless life leaving them empty and unfulfilled.

Overview of their real story behind closed doors

Let's take off the mask or blow away the smoke screen to see the truth of this family's life. Marv and Janice are devoted with their responsibilities of work and providing for their children. But it all has evolved into a *disorganized façade*.

They go to church because that's how they grew up, and they want their children to be good people, to know God, and eventually to go to heaven.

Marv works long hours, but mainly it's so he doesn't have to go home so soon and get in the middle of the storm with the kids and Janice. The needed raise is true, but it's more important to support his ego and hobbies, buying expensive man toys, and paying off Janice's shopping addictions.

Most of the shopping she does is for herself, to buy new clothes and things a couple of times a week to feel good about herself, because she believes she deserves it.

Janice goes to the gym early in the morning because she knows that Marv is at home and has to watch the kids until she gets back, which is security for her, so she can safely flirt with the guys that are continuously paying attention to her.

The computer games take Marv away from reality, with gaming being his legal drug. Then the computer turns into his mistress at night when Janice to goes to bed, so he can fantasize and watch pornography.

Their kids have taken over the house and their family life in general. Marv and Janice are devoted providers for their children, but have given up on their parental leadership responsibility, convincing themselves it's easier to be the kids' friends instead of parents. The children dictate what, where, and when things go on inside and outside the house most of the time. The kids are in control, not the adults, as boundaries and discipline don't seem to exist.

Marv's game playing, computer relationships, and weekend warrior stuff, along with Janice's inappropriate visits to the gym, excessive salon pampering appointments, and shopping are things that are being used to have satisfying identities outside the marriage. Not to mention discarding their responsibilities of being honorable and respectable parents.

Subconsciously, they are doing these, and many other extra things, to get lost in another world or reenact days gone by. Artificially creating false identities, mental pictures, or physical illusions to feel good, important, and valued.

With all this said, we haven't even scratched the surface about their social networking habits. Facebook, Instagram, Pinterest, Twitter, texting, and all the other things they believe are so essential, that they're willing to tally up countless hours in their day and night to make themselves feel part of a bigger and better family, to again, have fulfilling relationships, as well as to feel good, informed, important, and valued.

This fast paced, fully packed, insignificant, artificial lifestyle, filled with selfishness that is masking reality, is a deadly predator and is destroying families left and right. One that lies to us constantly that we can create our own ultimate fulfillment if we would only focus on number one (me) and do what makes me happy and feel good.

The order of life's priorities is all over the map with this family, and scrambled up so much, every relationship—the marriage, children, work, activities, and God—leave failure as the only destiny they have.

A. How many parts of this scenario rings true in your family?

Scenario #2
'Too committed'

"Sorry honey, I've got to go. You and the kids are going to have to have dinner without me tonight. I just got off the phone with Jim from church, and he and Staci are having troubles again. He called to see if I could come over and mediate between them over this big fight that they're in right now. It sounds pretty bad," Mike said to his wife Stephanie, walking into the kitchen as she was fixing dinner.

"But you just got home. You've been working all day," Stephanie said disappointedly, but not surprised.

"I know, but I have a never-ending job."

"When are you ever going to say no, and start being a part of your own family?" she questioned in a firm tone, as she turned from the stove and looked at him straight in the eyes.

"Come on, Stephanie, don't start this again."

She slammed her hand on the counter as she started to cry, saying, "I'm not the one starting anything. You do this to us all the time! You have all the time in the world for your church family, or everyone else for that matter. But your own family, flesh and blood, gets the backseat, the leftovers, and I'm sick and tired of it.

"The boys spend more time playing video games alone, or at the neighbor's house playing baseball with John and his kids in a week than they get to see and play with their own father in two months."

Mike walked up to Stephanie and gave her a hug, trying to console her, but she backed up and shrugged his arms off. "Mike, I'm tired! I'm so tired of being last on your list. Everyone else and their problems are your first priority. I'm almost convinced that we're here only for decoration as a perfect family, so you look good, as I'm only here to fix you food, raise your kids, and every night you have someone to share a bed with."

"How dare you say something like that, Stephanie. You and the kids are my life, and you know that, but my job is very important and takes up a lot of time. It's my responsibility as the pastor of our church to be there when someone needs me."

"So, we're your life...but if someone else needs help, you leave us for them. We're your life...but your job is so important that you'll sacrifice us so you do a great job and take care of their needs. We're your life...but because you're a leader of a church, the church family

21

and job are more important than your relationship with your own wife and kids!" She was talking louder and louder.

"Stephanie, keep it down the kids might hear us arguing," he said motioning downward with his hands.

"Are you serious, Mike? Are you that blind? The kids know exactly what is going on, and have for years. We've been over this a thousand times, and you just don't get it. I am tired..." She hesitated, still crying, and put her hand to her mouth. She calmed down and continued, "I am tired of our children not having a father around. I'm tired of *not* having my husband involved in my life or even having a husband at all." She patted her chest when she made the last statement. "Mike, I am so alone. I'm going through life as if you or our marriage is only a memory. The kids..." Stephanie leaned over to the edge of the counter where the tissue box was, grabbing one out, then whipped her eyes. "Mike, the kids have stopped asking where you are or when you're going to be home. You might as well be off in a faraway land, permanently doing missions by yourself.

"Do you know Billy is going fishing with John and his kids this weekend, and he didn't think of asking if you wanted to go? Do you know why? Because he knows his dad will not be around because he's out doing something for, or with, someone else's family. Billy knows he's not one of the important people in his dad's life."

She stepped forward just a few inches from Mike and put her hands up to his chest. She gently patted and rubbed her hands around, then dropped them down and took ahold of his hands. She looked down at their hands sniffling, then let go, stepping back, and looked up into his eyes saying, "You have a mistress in your life, and it's your precious job. To me it feels like you are continuously committing adultery."

"What?" Mike said as his heart sank.

"I'm pretty sure you're not having an affair with another woman. But how you treat our marriage, you might as well be. You never talk about us; your conversation is always about someone else. I'm not on your mind, and for that matter, I don't think I'm in your heart anymore."

"Stephanie?" He grabbed at her hands in desperation knowing she was relationally falling away from him. "You can't mean what you're saying. You know I love you! Sweetheart, listen to me, I love you and the kids so much, you have no idea. I'm working so hard every day to do God's work, which he called me to do. You know that, you were there with me in seminary. You took on the call with me, you knew then, and you know now, how difficult this position is for a leader of a church."

Stephanie replied, "It's difficult because you're doing it by yourself. You think that you've become the guardian angel or the Holy Spirit for everyone, and now no one can make a move in life without your help. You have handicapped the church and yourself by thinking you are able to fix all the problems of this world in the name of Jesus. But you have left out what our lives are completely about: that Jesus is the problem solver. Your job is to point everyone to Him to fix, or more accurately, to lead them through their journey of problems, so He can grow His relationship with them through their hurdles and situations."

Stephanie turned away and walked to the sink looking down, then added, "Mike, I'm leaving you and taking the kids to my mom's house. This has gone on for so long, and I've tried over and over to get your attention, and I don't know what to do anymore. It's come to the point that I don't know if I even want this relationship any longer. I need to clear my head, but most of all, my heart. It's become hardened towards you over the years, and it's going to take time to soften it again."

He stood there with his mouth wide open in surprise then said, "This can't be happening." He quickly walked to her and gently took her hand again and said, "Stephanie wait, I'll change, I'll start saying no. Please don't leave, we can work this out."

"Mike, it's too late."

"It's never too late. Come on, give us another chance."

She jerked away from him and stated aggressively, "Another chance? You want another chance? I gave us another chance hundreds of times, and you never have listened before. Maybe this time you'll finally hear and see clearly what the problem is." She pointed hard at his chest and said slowly and loudly, "Your problem is that your work is more important than your wife and kids! Your precious job is your number one priority over any relationship you've got, period. Even with your own personal relationship with God!"

Overview

In this scenario, we used a church leader to illustrate a very common hurdle with any career or activity in a marriage. But you can fill in the blank with you and/or your spouse's job, activities, or anything else that steals all your time, becoming your master, and you'll have the same result. We have been here and have experienced it firsthand.

Most people want to do their best to succeed in their careers, or even with other relationships, such as with their activities (hobbies, sports, entertainment, etc.). But blindly, one of these starts taking the wrong spot in the order of priority in our life, only to become destructive, unproductive, and ultimately becoming their god/master, taking the place of the true living God, the Master of the universe.

B. Have you experienced a time when you were "at the end of your rope" in a relationship?

C. Are you so focused on something it consumes every thought or all your time?

Scenario #3
'The Stand Off'

Jerry and Lori have been married for twenty-nine years. Their next-door neighbors, Steve and Gale, have been married thirty-two years.

Both couples raised their kids the best they knew how with all they had, just like most parents. Their kids are now gone and have children of their own. It's fun when they all get together; it's loud, and things are always happening. But when the children and grandchildren leave, both couples are alone together...again.

Jerry and Lori have a routine of a monotone and predictable relationship. It's always quiet between them, and for the most part uneventful. After work they eat dinner and watch television until its late, then it's time for bed.

They're always together, but live a lonely life. They do love each other, but the love isn't like that intimate love they had in their early years; it's love by habit. With the children gone, they find themselves with very few things in common anymore, as the majority of their interests have drifted apart.

Every Saturday morning, Gale goes over to have coffee with Lori, with Gale doing most of the talking.

"Lori, you wouldn't believe Steve. He's got another project in the garage that's taking up every evening. That man is constantly busy doing his own thing. He rarely does anything with me, or spends time with me like he used to. It's like he's purposely doing something to have an excuse to not be with me."

Lori thought to herself, *Jerry spends most of his time with me, but he might as well be doing something else. Our life is dull and we have very little conversation, or things in common for that matter.*

Gale continues, barely stopping to take another breath, "And he's planning another fishing trip with his buddies next weekend; he's always going somewhere. I just don't understand him. Oh well, I'm out and about doing my own things all the time anyways, so I guess we're even. How do you and Jerry do it?"

"Do what?"

"How do you and Jerry get along so well? You both are always together. Your house is quiet and you look happy, never arguing about anything. What's your secret?"

Lori thought to herself again, *Happy? Is this what you call happy?* Then replied, "Well, we don't make waves in our relationship. If Jerry or I have something to say, we do it quietly and kindly. If there is a problem, we usually just keep it to ourselves because eventually, over time, it goes away."

"You can do that? Just let things slide by without discussing it or hashing it out?" Gale said, frowning in disbelief.

Lori tilted her head back and forth, thinking about the question, then answered, "We don't have a lot to talk about. But if we do, and don't agree with each other, we don't make mountains out of mole hills. Why make waves when things usually just drift away on their own."

"Wow, I wish Steve and I could do that. All we do is argue and yell at each other most of the time."

I know, we can hear you two every day and night, Lori thought to herself as Gale continued, "So, you're telling me, just sweep it under the rug. Hide from everything, and turn your back and ignore it and it will all go away?"

Lori sat there frozen in thought as the words, 'hide from everything and turn you back and ignore it,' struck her hard. She just realized, that's what their relationship was all about- ignoring and hiding from everything. Even if it was confrontational or not, it would all just go away. The thought stabbed her heart, knowing that's what has happened to their loving marriage. It has faded away.

Gale blurted out, "There is no way Steve and I could do that. We get everything out in the open until one or the other gives in. Steve thinks he knows everything and tries to run me and the house. But I don't think so." Gale sat back in her chair folding her arms across her chest. "I'm my own woman, and if he thinks he's going to get his way, then he's got another thing coming, the idiot."

Overview

These two marriages have the same problem, just with different personalities and different ways to communicate. It's very sad to see many marriages or relationships like this, and they are everywhere. Especially when we get older and life becomes a stalemate.

How come their marriages lost purpose and have no obvious fulfillment from being together? Why didn't they naturally grow towards each other, getting stronger and better over time, like wine? Becoming distant relationally, getting farther apart, and aiming in different directions? Or maybe, they got into different ruts within their marriage, and are still going the same direction, but alone like the old wagon train trails with parallel deep tracks in the road.

More than likely their relationships had started growing apart early in the marriages, or jumped over into a different track over the years, and never realized it until their children left the house. Only later on, figuring it out that they had become completely different people with different interests, goals, and purpose?

D. Are you in a stalemate with your marriage?

E. Are you married, but feel alone?

These are fictitious stories we made up. Or are they? We could write books full of stories like these that have many different scenarios which we have experienced ourselves, or have seen many other families experiencing: nasty divorces, painfully losing a child, carrying past baggage, life at home with a veteran having P.T.S.D., living with a debilitating disease, having a pregnant teenager, a parent in prison, adultery, a parent or child addicted to drugs or alcohol, and on and on.

We have been married for over thirty years, and God has matured and directed our steps to be examples and get involved with marriages that He puts in front of us. Overwhelmingly, we have seen a large majority of couples that could slide into one of these scenarios and say, "Yes, that's us!"

Let's move forward and look into the multiple relationships we have in our lives that need to be put back in order. They're all the same for everyone!

Chapter 3

The Secret

*

"I can't wait to start *fixing* my husband/wife. Even those wild animals we call children, that terrorize our home. I sure hope you can also fix my stupid job situation. But I don't understand why putting our relationships in order has anything to do with fixing our problems and/or family. By the way, what are all these relationships you keep talking about, Mr. and Mrs. Crager?"

*

We're *not* talking about *fixing* someone. We are talking about first, finding out what the different relationships in our lives are. Then prioritize them in an order of importance, so we can finally see clearly what's causing the frustration, pain, and chaos, so that we can begin healing and moving forward. Once at this point, we'll finally have a compass to give us direction and a starting point, as well as a refreshed vision of purpose within all the relationships and in our own lives. This will finally lead us to enjoying life as our heart's desires begin to be filled, and *hope*—maybe for the first time in your life—moves forward to lead the way.

The individuals, circumstances, or obstacles that need to be *fixed*, as you stated, will automatically identify themselves as the weak or problematic areas that will systemically go into a reconstruction mode to start making forward progress. The majority of the time, this happens naturally on its own, after our relationships are in order.

But we will preface, *fixing the issues* will always need extra assistance here or there, along with the Fruits of the Spirit leading the way in our hearts and mind.

"But the Holy Spirit produces this kind of fruit in our lives: love, joy, peace, patience, kindness, goodness, faithfulness, gentleness, and self-control. There are no laws against these things" (Galatians 5:22-23). We will also add forgiveness because God forgave us, and does without ceasing. "Make allowance for each other's faults, and forgive anyone who offends you. Remember, the Lord forgave you, so you must forgive others" (Colossians 3:13). And sometimes, the thorns in our lives many never go away.

> [Apostle Paul] Three different times I begged the Lord to take it away. Each time he said, "My grace is all you need. My power works best in weakness." So now I am glad to boast about my weakness, so that the power of Christ can work through me. That's why I take pleasure in my weaknesses, and in the insults, hardships, persecutions, and troubles that I suffer for Christ. For when I am weak, then I am strong.
>
> 2 Corinthians 12:8-10

Life can suddenly get out of order, or as we sometimes see it, broken, and we didn't even know it until it was too late. Especially if

we never knew or were taught there was an order of importance with all the relationship in our lives. We can just see it, can't you? Our lives have turned into chaos, and we shout out into a large crowd of relationships, "Everyone in the pool!"

And before we know it, we can hardly move around, as we bump into one another with splashing and yelling going on loudly and uncontrollably.

Adding to that visual, it's so crowded and loud that we can't recognize who these people (relationships) are anymore, and we can't tell the difference if someone is yelling for help, or having fun. Until again, it's too late.

That's a sad picture but you know as well as we do there is always some type of carnage or wreckage when our lives get out of control, which started when we let it get *out of order.*

A. **Before thinking about what might need to be** *fixed* **with your spouse, career, children, and activities, consider first, the things your spouse or others might suggest need to be** *fixed* **with you and all your relationships.**

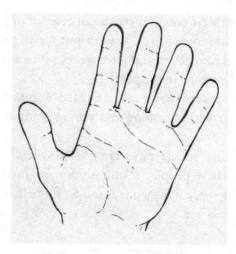

To make it easy, we will narrow down all the relationships we have into five categories, and for the moment they are in no specific order.

First, we'll start with the *relationship with our children, family and friends*. In this category, for simplification and understanding for those with or without children, we're going to *add all* extended family members, as well as friends.

Second, our *career relationship*. And why not? We spend at least one third to half our lives working, which affects all aspects of our lives and relationships, depending on how we let it control and affect our daily journey.

Third, the *relationship with God*. Are you a new believer or have you been a Christian all your life? Or maybe you have never had a relationship with the Creator God. Maybe you have a different type of god or master in your life that you could categorize having a relationship with in this category. For example: your job, Buddha, money, video games, sports, a political leader or political party, sex, social media, your car, even fear and worry, and so on. There is a plethora of things that can be your god, and one specifically is very strong; selfishness. It's all about you and your needs, wants, or desires, so you attempt to control and bully everything and everyone. But, for this book, *Is Your Life Out of Order?*, we are talking about the one true God, the Alpha and Omega, Jesus Christ.

Fourth, we'll follow that up with *activities relationship*, such as: hobbies, video games, reading, watching television, sports, hunting, fishing, shopping, social media, and last but not least, ministry.

Ministry has a different meaning than a relationship *with* God. It's a common mistake. We may ruffle some feathers and get a few disagreements by putting ministry in this category. But many times, we start worshiping or prioritizing the ministry and not God, or put the ministry before our personal relationship with God, thinking that's what having a relationship with God is (doing ministry). That is a false concept, and we can imagine God rolls His eyes at us when we think we are doing His will or a favor by uplifting our works before lifting up our praises and worship to Him for what He does for us.

We have seen, more times than not, long-time awesome fellow believers or newcomers to the family of God, leave the church or fade away from God. When the stigma, human expectations, or church leadership isn't careful, excessive ministry can put relationships out of order, which only damages the individuals and church family. This ultimately leads to relational and spiritual hurdles, but mostly *burnout*. Burnout with the church, and sadly burnout with God, who clearly had *nothing* to do with the low human understanding of what having a relationship with Him truly is and His expectations from us doing ministry.

Finally, *the marriage relationship*: the relationship with our spouses, the ones we married for sickness and health, for richer or poorer, to death do us part. More than likely, if you are reading this book, it's the main relationship you're focused on, and desiring the most to fix, or more accurately, put back in order. At least, that's what you *think* is the only one that needs to be put back in order.

B. What's the one main thing that has changed in your relationship since the day you got married to now?

C. What was your expectation of where your marriage would be right now when you got married?

D. For those not married, what is the one main unexpected change that has happened in your life?

Are you craving for your marriage to get back to where it was—loving and satisfying—where each cared deeply for the other and treated one another as though you were a queen or king, while your needs socially, emotionally, sexually, financially, spiritually, etc., were being fulfilled?

Perhaps you never started the marriage this way, and after the honeymoon there was no order at all. Subsequently, you are at your wits end to make sense of why you're married in the first place because the relationship is awful, painful, has no purpose or direction, and you're very unhappy and unfulfilled, with no hope in sight.

We all desire that our relationships function smoothly, and grow to enjoy and love each other more and more. Almost every morning when I (D. L.) open my eyes and see my wife (Shelly) sleeping next to me, I say to myself more often than not, "I love her more today, than I did yesterday." No joke, it's the truth. In my heart, looking past the quarrels, disappointments, and brokenness of this world and us—which come and go—I truly mean it, and my heart is at peace. My physical, emotional and spiritual needs and desires are content.

Life has direction and purpose in our awesome journey.

If your desire is to be able to say, "I love him/her more today than I did yesterday," then *you are* absolutely reading *the right book*!

E. Has your love grown or changed in an unexpected direction with your spouse since your got married?

Do you want to know the *secret* why we love each other more every day? It's not because my wife is hot (although she is). It's not because she fulfills my needs (although she absolutely does). It's not because she's an awesome cook (which is the reason for my happy belly) or that she has an important and cool career, or because she's the best mom or grandma.

It's not because my husband is a good man, dad, or grandpa, or that he's always been a hard worker and great leader, making sure we are financially secure, or, that he's faithful and treats me like his queen and is always attentive to my needs.

The secret is *simple*. We know where our marriage relationship is *positioned*, in comparison to our other relationships, and understand with it being in that *specific* slot of priority, our marriage continues to get better, like fine wine. And we'll confidently tell you...it *all* gets better, men and ladies, when our relationships are in order!

*

In addition to putting our lives/relationships in order, below are *five powerful intellectual and emotional lubricants* we highly encourage you to consider applying and injecting into your five relationships that will *strongly* assist for smoother and more insightful performing relationships once you get them *in order*.

1. Here's something important we need to bring into the picture to have great relationships. Would you not agree that *putting extra effort, hard work, consistent prayer, and going the extra mile* in everything we do, is vital to achieve success and be extraordinary? Most people do ordinary, and to be honest, we are *not* interested in ordinary. To us, ordinary is lazy, easy, and totally unfulfilling, mainly because we have

an *extraordinary God* that does extraordinary things, which shows us that extraordinary is achievable through Him. So, we strive for *extraordinary in everything* He has blessed us with, which includes all of our relationships. This is one of the reasons we wrote this book. Not only to bring awareness that we need to prioritize our relationships, but to help guide others to have extraordinary relationships as well, *not* plain and ordinary ones. Life is hard work if you like it or not, no question!

F. **Are you seeking after extraordinary, or are you just satisfied with ordinary?**

2. Another thing we have done, was *research each other's personality types, communication styles, and love languages.* These will help you understand how the other person naturally communicates, processes, and thinks because we can almost guarantee, everyone does these differently, one way or another. There are plenty of great resources out there to help you accurately understand how you, your spouse, children, and co-workers tick. If you want to make the interaction between yourself and others harmonize better

and rise to a higher level of meaning and enrichment, then *do your homework* about yourself and each other. Find out who you are and who your spouse and children are individually! We can't compare an apple to a banana to an orange, even though they are all fruits!

G. Are you and your spouse similar fruits? How are you different?

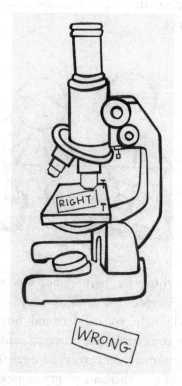

3. Here is something that is hard to do at first, but is very potent in a successful relationship. *Loosen up and let go of what you perceive is wrong about the other person, and focus*

and encourage them with what is right about them. Again, this is not only for married couples, but vital for parents and can be used at the workplace. Just think if everyone encouraged and applauded you all the time with what you do right, instead of painfully poking you in the eye all the time with what's wrong with you. How would you feel? You would always feel better about yourself, and have a better attitude to ultimately succeed at a higher level in all you do and who you are. Continually looking through the lens of what's wrong, is like looking out the backdoor of life—it's history and is an anchor—you'll never get anywhere. However, looking through the lens of what's right, is like looking through the front door of life—the future with sails opened wide—you'll move forward with new positive possibilities!

H. What are three things you really appreciate about your spouse?

4. For the next intellectual and emotional lubricant, we have a powerful saying we constantly tell people to quickly get them focused and realigned:

Unmet expectations lead to disappointment and frustration.

This means that when our *expectations are too high*, or our *plans do not go exactly as we wanted, disappointment and frustration* will continually be our friend, like it or not.

For example, men, when we create all these expectations throughout the day of what we want the bedroom scene to look like tonight with our wives, and it doesn't happen, or to the *circus*-level we created in our heads, what happens? We are disappointed and frustrated.

Ladies, when we plan and formulate things we expect from our husbands and they don't get done or go the way we wanted it, what happens? We are disappointed and frustrated.

We need to interject something vital here while we're on this topic, zeroing on the marriage. We're talking to husbands and wives equally. If we continually disappoint and deny one another the very needs that God created within us, we can almost guarantee the world's brokenness and darkness will step in psychologically, emotionally, but most of all, physically to satisfy those needs that male and female alike (but in different ways or areas) have a constant thirst and desire to be quenched.

The easy one: men. God purposely created men to have a strong external sexual drive; it's natural. You're not perverts or sick, unless you have an unhealthy addiction to sex. Wives, if this constant drive is not being taken care of by you, and with a loving and willing heart—don't make your man feel bad or guilty—a war within your husband will rage on beyond anything you could imagine. He is battling something that always will be hopeless to him. A man has the urge for sexual release approximately every 3 days, even though he's thinking about it 24 hours a day. Help him to stay focused on you, because if you don't, something on the computer or someone else could catch his eye or pay attention to him, and you'll have another battle on your hands.

The hard one: women. God purposely created women to have a strong internal emotional drive. It's one that is easy to oversee—out of sight, out of mind—but yet hard to explain. Men, it has all the same components of what we said about you, but it's with her heart that drives her crazy. The yearning that wives have for their husbands to caress their hearts with conversation, compassion, complements, attention, honesty, and romance would blow your mind. If you don't take care of it, and we'll repeat what we said above for men, with a loving and willing heart—don't make them feel bad or guilty—again the world could come at her from all directions to have those things satisfied through romantic books, movies, social media, or when someone else fills her heart's cup, and it's not her husband, a new battle is born.

There are plenty of books out there to help us in these areas, and it does take some honest and open communication, patience, and work. But if we consistently take our spouse's needs seriously and passionately, as we want our needs taken care of, there will be balance within this intimate loving relationship that will naturally find contentment.

"Do to others as you would like them to do to you" (Luke 6:31). This means that if you want your needs to be met, meet the needs of your spouse—God's perfect balance. "So again I say, each man must love his wife as he loves himself, and his wife must respect her husband" (Ephesians 5:33).

We need to be aware of our expectations of one another and how we plan for things. Are they realistic, or are we being like a straight and dry spaghetti noodle that has very little to no flexibility, and when slightly bent, it shatters into pieces? Or, are we being like a wet spaghetti noodle that can bend into many shapes without breaking, and is more tasteful?

No matter how hard we try to make our world to be heaven on earth, we will always fail in the area of having expectations of a perfect life and family portrait, because humanity is broken, and always will be. *Unmet expectations lead to disappointment and frustration.*

I. What expectations do you have that often lead to frustration?

5. This leads us to an elusive one: *who's your master?* This one is slithery, when many times we don't realize it until someone else brings it up, that we *have the wrong master controlling our lives.*

A master is something or someone we put our attention, loyalty, trust, investment, and expectations into for success, happiness, and hope. I'm not only talking about your bank account, your retirement fund, your job, a president, a political party, sports, science, living in the right city or neighborhood or attending the perfect church, or having your kids in the perfect school.

A master can be anything to anyone including fear, worry, eating right or wrong, staying healthy or unhealthy, working out, sex/lust, excessive admiration for someone, a pet, music, shopping, sports activities, gaming, alcohol or drugs, social media, and so on and so on.

Fill in the blank for yourself and your spouse of what is so *important*, and has become the master of your lives. To help you figure that out, answer these simple and possibly painful questions:

J. What are all the so-called important things you do every day?

K. How much time do you spend on each of these important things every day? Why?

L. Are these things honestly so important that you are willing to sacrifice important family relationships?

43

We have a different question for the consequences of who is your master. It's about *your legacy*. Picture yourself on your death bed. How will these so called "important" things that become masters in your life, contribute to your life story? How would they hypothetically be written on your tombstone or in your obituary?

Are you going to have traumatizing regrets? What images are you going to die with that tell the story of who you were, to your family and friends? Your loved ones, by the way, will talk about you after they have put you six feet into the ground, we guarantee it!

It could be, "Thank goodness they're dead; what a wasted life. He/she sure loved themselves and money, and never spent time with their family. They had no purpose and made nothing of their life. They had the opportunity to be an awesome friend or father/mother, but..."

Or, it could be a completely different story with your family and friends, as they imagine and celebrate you hearing from God when you approach Him at the pearly gates, *"Well done, fine and faithful servant! Come on in, let Me show you your mansion!"*

The Master we're leading you to, and who we need to focus on, is the Creator of the Universe—God. This leads us to start prioritizing our five relationships and understanding why they need to be in the order they are meant to be in, so we may begin to minimize the confusion, frustration, and heartaches, and *start living a thriving life of purpose that is in order.*

M. What or who has been your master/Master?

Chapter 4

Who's Leading

We have identified 5 relationships:

Children, family, and friends

Career   **Marriage**

God   **Activities**

Now let's begin to put them in their appropriate order of importance for an organized, balanced, joyful, and content life. Out of all these five, by now you probably know from how we've been talking, and what your heart is telling you, which is number one.

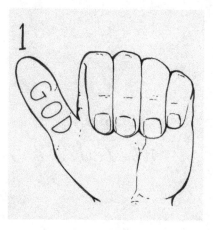

Yes, it's God. It *is* that obvious, and we intellectually and spiritually know it to be true because we know of Him in our hearts.

They know the truth about God because he has made it obvious to them. For ever since the world was created, people have seen the earth and sky. Through everything God made, they can clearly see his invisible qualities—his eternal power and divine nature. So, they have no excuse for not knowing God.

Romans 1:19-20

Why do we continually—consciously or subconsciously—drop God down in our priority list of relationships? There are *many* reasons we do this, but we're going to focus on three specific areas: communication, trust, and love.

1. *Communication* – We stop communicating with God!

We might think about God, talk about God, tell people we'll pray for them, but do we really interact with God? Even though we think about Him, are we actually communicating with Him?

Communication is a two-way street. How do we expect to hear from God, unless we pray directly to Him, and read

His living words from the Bible? Just thinking about God or talking about Him with other people is not communicating *with* Him.

The other half of the communication process is the willingness to wait patiently while *listening* for Him. There are many ways Jesus talks to us:

- *Through dreams* – Genesis 41, Daniel 2

- *In our hearts through the Holy Spirit* – Matthew 10:20, Acts 1:2, Romans 8:26-27

- *Through all of our situations and circumstances* – Stories throughout the Bible

- But most of all, when we *read the Bible*, His living Word – 2 Timothy 3:15-17, 2 Peter 1:16-21, Revelations 22:17-19

If we don't read the Bible, how are we to hear, know, and understand God and our relationship with Him? If we don't pray to Him, how are we to get a response, encouragement, or direction? If God wants to speak to us, He'll speak, but we make it hard on ourselves when we *do not* put forth effort to pick up the Bible or use the spiritual phone by praying and communicating with Him.

Do you not pray because you don't know how or what to say? Is prayer difficult because you don't know when or where to do it? Does it seem awkward because you feel you're just talking to yourself or into thin air?

We all have to start sometime and somewhere, and right now would be a great time to start. The best example of why prayer is important, is with Jesus in the first four books of the New Testament in the Bible. He was born the Son of God and Savior of this world, but He still prayed continually, and with great passion and dedication. He knew then that the intimate, emotional, and spiritual communication with His Father—God—was the most essential connection, daily discipline, and strongest building block He needed for His humanity in His daily walk.

The fruits that come because of this discipline (comfort, peace, love, protection, strength, and direction) greatly blessed Him, and are equal gifts to us if we only would spend time with God, talking back and forth. *There is no relationship without communication*, and if you are not communicating with God, you have no relationship with Him. He's waiting on us!

To help guide you to begin praying, we learned long ago to hypothetically break prayer down into five segments, which are in a certain order to keep us on track to be respectful and have more understanding of our relationship with our Lord.

First, in your own words *acknowledge God*, who He is in your life, and how great He is as the Creator of the Universe. This helps us keep Him in the forefront of our lives, continually reminding us that we are the created, when the world is constantly telling us to selfishly look out for ourselves and always be number one.

Second, give thanks to God for what He has done. There are more things He has done for us than we can count, but we easily forget because we get tunnel vision with what we want next in our selfish lives. We fall short with this one many times, and forget when a blessing happened in our lives. In the excitement, we leave out the only One qualified to bless us supernaturally.

Third, this is when we *present to God our requests and needs*. Putting them in this order (the back seat, per se) relationally helps us grow in more ways than we can understand. This order also helps us to stop using God as a Santa Claus. We know that sounds crude, but are we right? We humanly do it all the time, pleading and pleading for something, and if it doesn't happen or doesn't go the way we plan it to happen, we get discouraged, throw a fit, and get an attitude with God. We need to be reminded that we are the created, but are very loved at the same time by our Creator. If He didn't love us, He wouldn't have given us a second thought or the air to breathe.

Fourth, thank Him again, but in a different manor, for always having the time to commune with us, for what He is going to do in our lives in advance, and how He is going to answer our prayers. Remember, God knows us from all directions, time and place. He knows in detail every person on earth, and understands how to work for the good of those who love Him, according to His purpose. This purpose is ultimately loving His children, and for His children to love Him. So, no matter how prayers are or are not answered, our Lord and Savior will always have His best interests in mind—us, His children.

Fifth and finally, *pray and live with great expectations of what God is going to do.* This might not sound like prayer to you, but we live this in and out of our prayer lives. We believe our communion with God never ends. Many times, we don't say, "Amen," when finished praying, because it sounds so final/permanent, as if we turned off the phone, disconnecting all communication with Him. God is with us non-stop. The Holy Spirit is right by our side, going through life with us, knowing exactly where and when we are. So why act and pray as though He's stuck somewhere in the cosmos and we have to set up a satellite link—living a long-distance relationship with Him? We all know long-distance relationships *do not* last or work. Why do you think Jesus left the Holy Spirit to be with us here on earth in the first place?

A. Are you communicating with God daily?

B. Are you always trying to get something out of Him, or are you giving to Him?

2. *Trust* – Another reason God drops down our lists of relationships is because we stop trusting him.

"Trust is so hard to gain, but so easy to lose." We don't know who first quoted that, but we've all heard it. Many times, we lose our trust or faith in God because it didn't work out the way we wanted it, or something awful happened and we blame Him.

We stop trusting God because we start believing in our limited human understanding of Him and our vision of tomorrow. Our outlook gets clouded, as the evil one relentlessly pursues us, blowing lies of smoke into our minds.

God doesn't make or cause awful things to happen. Our broken and selfish humanity is why bad and imperfect things happen, which started with Adam and Eve. They chose to do the opposite of what God told them to do. It's like a parent telling their child not to do something, knowing clearly that if their child did do the thing they said not to do, it would have grave consequences they would have to live with.

We had to correct a friend the other day because he was saying to someone that was going through a painful and difficult situation, and we'll paraphrase it, "God wanted you to go through that. God puts trials in our lives so we..." you fill in the blanks. Bad, bad information and theology people! Especially in the timing of when we say these things for encouragement because we don't know what else to say. What an awful thing to say to someone that is hurting and needs comfort from us and our loving Lord Jesus, who knows the situation and them more intimately than we could fathom.

The bad statement above usually forms an invisible wall, which we build to separate us from God so He will not hurt us again, according to this skewed perspective. *It's lost trust and is hopeless.*

Let's compare that with a gentle and loving parent who would be there for their hurting child who had fallen over while learning to ride a bike. The parent did not make their child painfully fall; it just happened while learning to ride. If the parent never let go of the bike, the child would never learn to ride by themselves. The parent is helping and encouraging their child, because they want the best for them and believe their child can do it. Ultimately, it gives the child hope that they can do it. *This is strengthening trust and is hopeful.*

What is so ironic about trust, from God's perspective, is that it's the complete opposite with Him for us. Trust is easy and impossible to lose. You see, since He created us, He *believes* in us, which means He's for us to the end.

It doesn't mean He trusts that we will be perfect little religious soldiers or robots. His trust in us is His confidence for us that we have the ability to accept Him as our Savior. We need to begin or refresh our trust in Jesus, to keep Him in the number one spot of our relationships. That means to have faith and trust that He loves us no matter what, *through all the bad or good happening in our lives. It doesn't mean the bad things and pain will stop knocking on our door*; that's all natural in this imperfect world. It means that we can trust that *Jesus is the hope* in our lives that can bring joy in our hearts, knowing He loves us and has the ability to work all things for the good for the those who love Him who have been called according to His purpose.

Jesus says, "Don't let your hearts be troubled. Trust in God, and trust also in me" (John 14:1).

"We know dear brothers and sisters, that God loves you and has chosen you to be his own people" (1 Thessalonians 1:4).

I pray that God, the source of hope, will fill you completely with joy and peace because you trust in him. Then you will overflow with confident hope through the power of the Holy Spirit.

Romans 15:13

C. Can you clearly state that you trust God with all aspects of your life?

This leads to our third point of why we put God in the back seat of our lives so many times.

3. *Love* - We stop loving God.

Jesus replied, "The most important commandment is this: 'Listen, O Israel! The Lord our God is the one and only Lord. And you must love the Lord your God with all your heart, all your soul, all your mind and all your strength.'"

Mark 12:29-30

"But anyone who does not love does not know God, for God is love" (1 John 4:8).

"For God so loved the world that he gave his one and only Son, that whoever believes in him shall not perish but have eternal life" (John 3:16, NIV).

If that's not love, then we don't know what is! Is there anyone that would give their child's life for us? No! But yet we grasp ahold of anything or anyone that we perceive will give us happiness, pleasure, and satisfaction, as we let go of Jesus's hand. As this thing or person—which we can humanly feel with all our senses—ultimately *will only give us false illusion of forever fulfillment and security.* Because with our broken humanity and not being divine, *we wrap up our dreams and hope in the here and now, and stop thinking eternally (forever). That, our friends, is the "Achilles's heel" for many people.*

D. Do you love God above all other people, things, or ideals?

Is God out of sight, out of mind in our life?

God has not gone anywhere, we have!

We are the ones that turn away and let go of His hand!

When we lose sight of God being the most important relationship in our life, our interaction with Him *fades away.* He quickly gets crowded out and becomes invisible in our tangible and clouded world.

Pathetic? Absolutely! We do it all the time. When things start going good or bad, before we know it, we let go of His hand—communicating with Him—and start holding the hand of something else—a different master—that *we* put in His place.

He knows us inside and out. He knows our pains yesterday, today, and tomorrow.

"'I am the Alpha and the Omega—the beginning and the end,' says the Lord God. 'I am the one who is, who always was, and who is still to come—the Almighty One'" (Revelations 1:8).

But more importantly, He knows what our heart's desires are, and loves us so much that He wants to fill them. "He fulfills the desires of those who fear him; he hears their cry and saves them" (Psalms 145:19, NIV). "Take delight in the Lord, and he will give you the desires of your heart" (Psalms 37:4, NIV). God is the only one that can work all things—wrong, bad, and painful—for the good. "And we know that God causes everything to work together for the good of those who love God and are called according to his purpose for them" (Romans 8:28).

E. Do you have something else that is the "master" of your life besides God?

Have you ever been to a symphony? There is a reason that the conductor is up front leading, as all the musicians are watching and waiting for instructions from him. He has the knowledge and experience of every instrument and knows the composition in detail for each instrument to perfectly harmonize all at once with precise and perfect timing.

Why do we try to be the conductor and the musician in our lives, when we are only specific instruments in the orchestra of life? God is the only One that knows about our tomorrows. He intimately and individually knows our strengths and weaknesses, because He made us. So why do we think we can take His place and be our own conductor, when we have no clue of what is going to be on our future music sheets?

"Don't brag about tomorrow, since you don't know what the day will bring" (Proverbs 27:1).

"So don't worry about tomorrow, for tomorrow will bring its own worries. Today's troubles are enough for today" (Matthew 6:34).

"We can make our plans, but the Lord determines our steps" (Proverbs 16:9).

F. Have you ever come to realize that God can orchestrate our future path? Do you let Him be the conductor in your life?

*

"That sounds good and all that God is right for you, but He's not for me. I believe differently. I've given God a chance many times, but we just never saw eye to eye on things, or He never shows up. What He wants and what I want always seem to be two different things."

*

You believe whatever you want; we're free to choose. However, we are speaking to you from decades of personal experience, witnessing the living God work in our lives and thousands of others' lives. We have concluded all the other gods out there—including self-deity—

only leads to an empty and purposeless life with a hopeless end, so you choose. Which choice, by itself, is a gift from God. Just like with Adam and Eve when they got to choose to eat the apple or not, even when He warned them not to.

When God is first in all our relationships, we have set in play the *only* firm and eternal foundation there is known to man, strong enough to build all other relationships upon. Do we have to give up some of our skewed human thoughts or desires? Yes we do, and we do it by faith and not by our lowly understanding of why.

Let's not be like a child throwing a fit because we didn't get our way after our parents said no, or did something against what we wanted.

"When the earth quakes and its people live in turmoil, I am the one who keeps its foundation firm" (Psalms 75:3).

"Fear of the Lord is the foundation of true knowledge, but fools despise wisdom and discipline" (Proverbs 1:7).

When God is first in our hearts, the second relationship in order will be blessed, influenced, and will absorb the flow of love and wisdom that God brings into our lives, as it is strengthened to do the same thing for the third prioritized relationship, and so on.

G. Are you getting a clear picture that God has to be the first priority to have your life in order? What do you need to do to start putting God first?

Chapter 5

Catapult the Family

Since we have established that our relationship with God must be number one in our lives, we can move on to our second priority relationship, which is our *marriage relationship*.

Now for those that are not married—single or divorced—please keep reading because prioritizing relationships is for everyone. It is vital you understand the appropriate order of relationships if you remain single, or in case you are planning to get married (or remarried) someday. Also, if you're put in a position in which you need to help a friend that is going through tough times, you'll have a clearer understanding of how to help them put their lives in order.

If you are single or divorced, the relationship you would put in slot or priority number two is the relationship we have in the number three slot. So be flexible—like a wet spaghetti noodle—and make the easy adjustment.

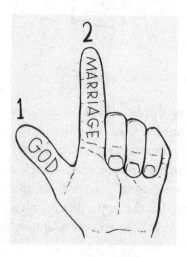

*

"So why is the marriage relationship second in order of the five? Don't we have more important responsibilities that depend on us than our spouses?"

*

Answering the next two questions will swiftly lead you to answer your own question.

- Which relationships in our lives have the ability to continuously mature and change, but will *not go* away because of time or age?

- Second, which relationships mature and change, and *will* go away because of time or age?

The *career relationship* changes for most people—not all—about every five to ten years. We change jobs for multiple reasons: better pay, hours, position, retirement, and so on.

The *activities relationships* change or go away continuously because of our age, expense, health, interests, family dynamics, geography, etc.

The *children, family, and friend's relationships* change and go away, just like our kids that grow up and move away and have families of their own.

> "Haven't you read," he replied, "that at the beginning the Creator 'made them male and female,' and said, 'For this reason a man will leave his father and mother and be united to his wife, and the two will become one flesh.'"
>
> Matthew 19:4-5 (NIV)

You see the picture. Our relationship with Jesus grows and changes as well as our marriage, but does *not* go away because of time or age. So obviously, our *marriage relationship* needs to be the second most important priority in our lives.

*

"That's nonsense! We need to be focusing on our children and their lives before ours! It's our responsibility as parents!"

*

If that's your thinking, you are absolutely setting yourself and your marriage up for failure and disappointment! You are looking through the *wrong* lens.

We're *not* saying love your spouse more than your children. It has nothing to do with the *volume* of love. It's the continual daily focus of caring and nurturing the marriage relationship and *not* putting it on hold *until* the kids are out of the house. Your marriage cannot afford to take a backseat for the children, careers, or activities relationships.

When your children see and experience their parents having an honest and purposeful loving marriage—believe me, they will know if you're faking it—you will have planted one of the most *powerful seeds* you can for them as parents to have the opportunity to pursue a wonderful marriage of their own.

Unfortunately, in our society today with the high divorce rate and disastrous marriages that are out of order, many children don't have a clue what a healthy relationship with Jesus and marriage is or looks like. Sadly, the odds are against them, and will possibly duplicate the same painful picture their parents had painted for them, having their own life and marriage out of order and in shambles.

A. Do you now believe that the marriage relationship needs to be in the second position, ahead of the others? Where has it been?

*

"You don't know my marriage or spouse or our kids. I (we) have tried to make it work, but it's not working."

*

We understand your frustration, but everything has to have a starting point. If we don't have a starting point, we will never begin the journey. We will always be in a gridlock only surviving, and that is no way to live. We all want to be thriving in life.

There is no better place to start, than first putting our life in order, to clear the chaos and clutter that is blinding us from identifying our relational injuries, hurdles, and circumstances, so that we may begin the healing process to get stronger and begin growing and thriving to have a balanced, joyful, and content life.

Let's go back to the three different marriage scenarios in chapter two. We could have written out a dozen more that were different, and have one that better fits your relationship. Then we listed out sixteen routine obstacles and hurdles, as well as situations and circumstances that could cause friction or disaster in relationships.

In chapter three, we explained five powerful intellectual and emotional lubricants to consider applying and injecting into your relationships, with chapter four focusing on God being number one in your life. And so far, there have been handfuls of motivating and valuable vitamins in between, that we could almost guarantee, has sparked your mind to start thinking deeper into specific areas for you and your spouse, that could transform your priorities and how your heart beats to have enriching marriages.

B. Let's stop and check in at this point. What are the specific helpful and encouraging vitamins have you grasped from the book so far that you're needing to help correct or refine your relationships to assist in getting your life in order?

Now, let's get a healthy perspective of *how* we start moving forward. Many times, it's *the small things* that will naturally turn into larger things as long as *the presentation was good, timely, and appropriate*. What do we mean by that?

We'll use fishing analogies.

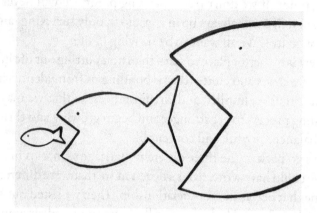

- *First,* only take on what you know you and/or they can handle at the moment. For example, a small fish will be eaten by a medium-sized fish, that will be eaten by a large fish, and so on. This is a simple way of growing and changing things, *one little step at a time,* so it will not be painful trying to swallow too much at once. Remember the statement, "Unmet expectations lead to disappointment and frustration."

- *Second,* your presentation will make it or break it. What, when, how, and how much you are presenting things to yourself, your spouse, and children is all very important! We would not go fishing in a small stream for brook trout and use a giant lure and heavy-duty rod and reel that would be used in the ocean fishing for marlin. The lure would be three times the size of the small fish as the rod and reel is overkill as well. Then trying to lug around the large and heavy tackle through the dense woods in the mountains would be a nightmare. Finally, you would not try to fish in the small stream in the middle of the winter, during a snowstorm, when the river was frozen over, and there was four feet of snow on the ground.

It's all wrong! Are you getting the picture?

Is it getting easier to absorb and understand how we are going to begin to move forward with all this information, catapulting our relationships towards balance, joy, and contentment as we put our lives in order?

Realistically, most everything is not going to improve instantly or to complete perfection. But by making the most important relational adjustment, by letting God be your number one relationship, we believe miracles can happen.

C. What small steps would you suggest making to begin the path towards putting your life in order?

Chapter 6

Give the Best Gift

We bet you can guess by now which relationship needs to be the third on the list of priorities in our lives: the children, family, and friend relationships.

The love we have for our children and family members is obviously great, and again, has *nothing* to do with the volume of our love. The love for God and our spouse is a different kind of love. One that is deep and intimate, created only for Jesus and our spouse.

"Husbands, love your wives, just as Christ loved the church and gave himself up for her" (Ephesians 5:25, NIV).

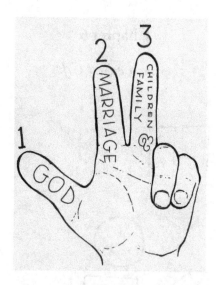

Having our children smack down in the middle of all five of our relationships is perfect! They have the ability from this perspective to look in both directions of their parents' lives and see what could be in store for them in their future. It's up to the parents to demonstrate and prioritize a balanced life in order, for them to have a vision, and the possibility and ability to have a joyful, content, and successful life of their own.

Parenting is an extremely heavy responsibility because we are their example and compass that point towards a healthy and purposeful future, or an unhealthy dead end with no future. When it comes time for them to make decisions on their own, how we are parenting and teaching our children has the ability to set them up to have a *life in order* so they may experience a balanced, joyful, and content life themselves. But most of all, we want them to understand and experience the love of God through their parents.

A. How would you say you are doing in this area? Are you modeling a life in order for your children?

B. Can your children—young or old—see their parents having a prosperous relationship with God?

God is to be our foundation and first-priority relationship in our lives. But, for an innocent and helpless child growing up until they come of age, we parents are, and need to be, their first foundation and a consistent foundation of love. All while being the representation of God and reflecting His character.

Coming of age is when they get to the point where they are able to logically, intellectually, and spiritually think and make decisions for themselves. It usually happens steps at a time, but eventually, it is all on their shoulders.

From this truth and perspective, how are we feeling about being parents and understanding why it's important and completely our responsibility to be their temporary foundation while they are young? It just got heavier, right?

As their temporary first foundation, again we're *not* saying be God to them, but be the ones to *introduce* them to the living God. What are they seeing and experiencing firsthand through their parents' lives, that Jesus is their true foundation and the ultimate foundation for everyone?

Are we introducing them to different priorities or masters before God, which could more than likely start their young lives completely *out of order*, only to struggle later on in life when relationships and responsibilities get piled on as they come of age and grow up? Let's take a moment and reflect back to our own childhood, who influenced us, and how.

C. Who influenced you in your life? What was it about them that makes you think of them as good or bad role models?

*

"I'm doing the best I can with where our marriage is at, and what I have to raise our kids with. What am I supposed to do, or not do, to be a better parent and give our children a chance of understanding life's priorities?"

*

Great question, but here's where we could walk into sinking sand. Jesus said, "But everyone who hears these words of mine and does not put them into practice is like a foolish man who built his house on sand" (Matthew 7:26, NIV).

We usually act or react from our own life experiences and how we grew up, good or bad. Then we are influenced by our society and culture, or what is popular in the parenting world, as though it's better and a new revelation. That last part of that sentence is a *joke* by the way.

How many times in the confusion of this world, even with good intentions, do we maintain the course of a child's life being out of order, or sway the pendulum *way too far* to the other side, so our children don't grow up like we did? Subsequently and subconsciously, we put ourselves in a spot and become somewhat their holy spirit to protect them and not let God be God.

*

"I don't understand, you just said that parents are to be their first foundation in their early years."

*

Yes, we did. And we followed that with the idea that we are to introduce them to God through our lives; not be God to them.

When Jesus saw what was happening, he was angry with his disciples. He said to them, "Let the children come to me. Don't stop them! For the Kingdom of God belongs to those who are like these children."

Mark 10:14

How we parent can be very simple, but we make it difficult because of a plethora of *stuff*!

We're going to explain four primary ways, out of many, that we parent to extremes. Which ones do you see yourself parenting to extremes that could mislead your children to possibly have a life out of order when they come of age?

1. *Hovering or sheltering parents* – Some parents become their child's shield in everything because of their lack of faith with fear nesting in their hearts, so they *excessively* protect their child from experiencing this world in any healthy manor. To understand firsthand what the difference is between right or wrong, and seeing Jesus in action—not mom and dad taking His place. How are you supposed to help train your children for a life—which is a constant battle of spiritual warfare—if you *only* tell them about the armor of God, but not how to use it?

> Therefore put on the full armor of God, so that when the day of evil comes, you may be able to stand your ground, and after you have done everything, to stand. Stand firm then, with the belt of truth buckled around your waist, with the breastplate of righteousness in place, and with your feet fitted with the readiness that comes from the gospel of peace. In addition to all this, take up the shield of faith, with which you can extinguish all the flaming arrows of the evil one. Take the helmet of salvation and the sword of the Spirit, which is the word of God.
>
> Ephesians 6:13-17 (NIV)

Not allowing our children to put the armor on and *train on the practice field* with their parents, until they are old enough to battle and defend themselves on their own, we will have set them up for *failure*. A majority of the time what happens with these children when they are finally able to get out from under their parents hovering over or keeping them boxed in all the time, they run away to the other side, ripping apart the hearts of their parents that love them so much. Unfortunately, you did not allow them to have minor personal experiences, as the old saying goes, "you fished for them and didn't teach them how to fish for themselves," so they may have a greater chance of spiritually floundering and putting their lives out of order.

D. Would you classify your parenting in this category? Do you hover too much, or do you provide them the tools to allow God to influence and direct them?

2. *The great giving parents* – These parents continually give their children, young and old alike, anything and everything, every time their children want or need something. First of all, we set them up for *failure* because they will always get what they want when they want it, spoiling them. Second, how are our children ever going to *grow* and experience *real life* by having nothing, a little or a lot, if all they've had is a lot of everything? When are they supposed to begin to trust God and experience Him—not their parents—when we continually get in His way putting Him in the back shadows of our lives? They need to experience Jesus firsthand at a young age, who is the ultimate and perfect Provider. Learning that He knows their tomorrows and knows them so intimately, that He can and will always provide exactly

what they need to continuously draw them closer to Him. We need to be careful not to put ourselves, the parent, as their *permanent* first relational priority—but God—for now, and later on as adults. We've seen it many times when adult children's parents pass away, and these adult children can never move forward—financially, emotionally, but most of all, spiritually—and blame God for taking them because He took their earthly god (provider) away, leaving them floundering, with a life out of order.

E. **Do you provide everything your children want? Have you taught your children the difference between wants and needs, while teaching them Jesus is the ultimate provider?**

3. *Parents with no boundaries* – This is where many parents are at with their children today, believing that life without boundaries will help them succeed, as boundaries only keeps their children caged in from reaching their potential. They also believe life with no boundaries is the child's *right*, as they should be able to choose and think for themselves what is right or wrong, no matter how old they are, or what little to no life experience they have, believing truth and lies equally. What's the saying? "If it feels good, do it and don't worry about the consequences." If you think this is right, you are *no* parent. The dictionary definition of a *parent* is, "one who gives birth, nurtures and raises a child, one who plays the role of guardian." If you *are* putting God in the first priority of your life and you have read the Bible, you know then, it's filled with boundaries.

"For God so loved the world that he gave his one and only Son, that whoever *believes* in Him will not parish but have eternal life" (John 3:16, NIV). The word "believes" in that powerful verse is a boundary. You must *believe in Him*, if you want to go to heaven when you die. That's a boundary. God gives us boundaries to instruct us, help us, discipline us, guide us, and love us. Without boundaries, well, we become our own god, and guess how that will end? The moral of this style of parenting is, life without boundaries completely goes against everything God teaches us. Which includes—hear us closely—*discipline and consequences*. Our children must know and understand there are consequences for every action they do, good or bad, that will affect them and their future. We must take the responsibility as parents and discipline our children because we love them. As you know, the outside world will discipline them void of care and love. Think about that! Don't let your child fail and flounder because you were scared; they may not like you for disciplining them. Later in life, they will see clearly and appreciate how their parents loved and protected them by having boundaries and being disciplined.

F. **Have you created clear, consistent, and fair boundaries for your children?**

4. *Shoveling and stomping parents* – These parents are usually on a completely unrealistic mission. A mission to shovel or force as much information, training or intelligence into their children, such as: doctrine, personal beliefs, opinions, religion, job skills, athletics, academics, etc. Parents think this is so important that a majority of these children end up *obese or drowning* emotionally, psychologically, physically, and spiritually. We're going to focus on religion. *Religion*...now that is definitely a sour word to identify what we have with God. So, let's scratch that, and put in the appropriate word,

relationship. Oh, what a coincidence, or is it, that that is what we've been talking about this whole time? Parents, we need to remember our children are *not* us and not our property. They are the property of God and are responsible for themselves when adults. God created them to be different and separated from their parents when they get older. We must learn balance and teach balance. Too much of one thing ruins a person. They will only know *one way* to act, think, and survive, and that would be their parents' way—not their own—with little to no influence of God. How is God supposed to work in their situations and hurdles with their different personalities, in a completely different location and era, if they can't take a step or know how to go a different direction when needed, if they only know one way? We're *not* talking about The Way, Jesus. This leads to our main point with the religion and relationship thing pertaining to God. If we only shovel knowledge and information *about* God down our child's throat all their lives, then *God will only be a religion to them.* Is that what we want or intended? No! Then let's be wise on how we raise our children to understand and know God so they will have a healthy relationship with Him, learning about Him through us. Just because our children *know of* God, definitely doesn't mean they *know* God. Satan knows God; that's why he attacks our children with a vengeance. We need to allow God to move freely within the family, through us, by reflecting and imitating Jesus. It's our responsibility, so He can touch each person individually. This means we need to maintain our course, guiding our children towards Jesus. Allowing flexibility—the spaghetti noodle concept—for God to work with and on our children at their level and pace, and for how they will grow and learn their relationship with Him, which will be different than ours.

G. Are you allowing or encouraging your children to grow and strengthen with their own personalities, talents, and skills that God blessed them with? Or have you been trying to live out your life through your child's life?

These are broad samplings of parenting styles to extremes. With many different hurdles and circumstances in our lives—too many to sift through in this book—we know there is a learning vitamin here and there that you can take to help move or improve your parenting. Even if it is only by *one percent*. Long term, that one percent could be huge years down the road for your children and you.

We have adult children and young grandchildren. Shelly has been in private Christian education for over twenty-five years, and most of those years a principal. Through those years we've heard hundreds, if not thousands, of stories—good and bad—pertaining to how parents attempt to raise their children. Many times, we just shake our heads and pray for these parents that are setting their children up for obvious failure.

It's never too late for us parents and our children. Remember us saying earlier that God constantly forgives us? Now picture a reset button for our lives, and push it now! First, put your relationships in order, adjust what and how you are parenting, then have a deep heart-to-heart talk with your kids, young or old, and enlighten them of your new parenting map and purpose. Then ask them to forgive you, if you have been leading them on the path to failure.

When children see firsthand that their parents are being true and honest, but most of all, continually *surrendering* to God, it will be another *great gift* a parent can give their children!

Chapter 7

Your Heart's Desire

The fourth relational priority is a struggle for many, but mostly men; it's our *career relationship*. This is an obvious and continuous problem in our lives today, and for most people, it will hit close to home.

Our career is our financial pipeline. Our career is how we classify ourselves professionally. Our career dictates how much time we spend with our families. Our career is what gives us identity. Our career helps us feel accomplishment and satisfaction.

*

"How in the world are we going to move our job into the fourth position of our relationships when it *controls* almost everything in my life and my family?"

*

Another great question. An easy, but yet hard, one. You said the key word, *control*! Most jobs are nine-to-five, Monday through Friday. If you are in this category, it's generally easier. If you are in a career that has three different shifts—day, swing and night—and goes on seven days a week, rotating days off, this is much more difficult, or is it? We also are in a changing society of mobile working, or working from home, which has its own dynamics.

We need to preface that in this chapter, we are focusing on our careers being out of order because they are out of control. The flip side to this is when we are lazy and not being responsible. We'll let the scripture below speak for itself.

> Make it your goal to live a quiet life, minding your own business and working with your hands, just as we instructed you before. Then people who are not believers will respect the way you live, and you will not need to depend on others.
>
> 1 Thessalonians 4:11

Here are some questions about your job we need to ask before going on:

- Are you always doing more or extra than what's required of you?
- Are you one that never says "no" when asked to do more than your normal duties?
- Are you working overtime, all the time?

- Are you addicted to your work?

- When was the last time you took a full vacation?

- Do you bring your work home or work extra hours when you don't need to?

- Do you put more faith in how much you do, and in your job, than what God can do?

- Do you worry that if you don't do the extras, you'll be replaced?

A. Which of these would describe your working habits? How long has it been going on?

Why do we do these things? To be responsible? Or...

✓ Afraid we will not make it financially or not get that raise or a promotion

✓ Afraid we will not be liked and appreciated at the work place

✓ Afraid we'll lose our job or be replaced

✓ Afraid we'll miss out on a client or something else at work

✓ To reach earthly goals and dreams

We can continue on and on, but we're going to pierce the main issue head on to quickly get to the point. Growing up in America, we have this saying "the American dream." For the most part, *everyone* has the opportunity to move towards their dreams, no matter who you are...*no excuses*.

We have seen many professional athletes that only have a high school education or less. We have seen managers and CEO's that only have a GED or high school education. We have seen successful business owners that only started with nothing or a few dollars to their name.

We know other true stories, like Helen Keller, being blind and deaf, but yet wrote books more than one hundred years ago. We know of people that were told they would never walk again, but are walking now. We know of people that were told they will die at a specific time because of a disease, but are still alive years later. We know it took Thomas Edison, and many other famous inventors, years and hundreds of attempts before their inventions became fully functional. There are thousands of stories from all walks of life, no matter your financial background, race, creed, nationality, age, gender, education, etc. that have accomplished their dreams.

All these people in many different situations, times, and places did not allow—figuratively speaking—storms, obstacles, hurdles, and circumstances to get in the way to accomplish their dreams. They did not stop moving forward when everything was against them: time, money, race, age, education, difficult and tough situations, and most of all, other people or society telling them they could not do it.

These accomplishments came true because of sheer will and determination, hard work, but most of all, *they had a dream*. We have heard this type of conversation or speeches many times which are inspiring to say the least. But we need to go beyond a dream, and understand what a dream really is. Which leads us more importantly to uncover specifically what is our *heart's desire*.

*

"What in the world are you talking about? I thought we were talking about our careers. I know what my heart's desire is. It's my dream; they're one and the same!"

*

We are talking about our careers; be patient. We also thought they were the same, until we figured out that our dreams and our heart's desires are two different things. Our dreams come from our minds, as our heart's desires come from our—wait for it—hearts. It's that simple.

Our dreams are created from what we have seen, heard, smelled, tasted, and touched—our senses—from the world. They are influenced or directed by our interests, personality types, talents, upbringing, past experiences, culture, and society.

Our heart's desire is planted the moment we were conceived. It is a gift we are given by God, which most of the time, as we have eluted to, is unfortunately confused and interpreted as one of the same with dreams.

You see, when we finally understand what our heart's desire is, our dreams will align with God and will be fulfilled in ways we cannot comprehend, in ways of the supernatural, *not* by our own doings or understanding. When we experience this, the extraordinary always follows.

Dreams will come and go. Once we accomplish a dream, one of two things happen; it's all downhill from there, or we dream another dream again, trying to fill *another* void, repeating itself over and over. Many times with dreams, we are disappointed because when we finally reach them, it wasn't all that we had envisioned or planned it to be. Dreams usually involve money, power, title, or pleasure: inward, selfish accomplishment.

Once our heart's desire is understood, *contentment* will always be there. It will never go away or be emptied. The heart's desired destination is having an eternal purpose and drive that is inspired by God to be enjoyed *with* Him, experiencing moments and things that go beyond our imagination. That means it goes further than we can dream. Our heart's desires usually involve doing things not only for ourselves, but mostly for helping others in a plethora of ways: outward, unselfish accomplishments.

Our dreams will always come and go, or come to a dead end and be a *was*... With our heart's desire, it is never ending and will always be an *is*...

When our heart's desire is understood, joy will begin to blossom and contentment will be our friend, because we are basking in a *relationship, not a selfish worldly accomplishment.*

We're not saying to stop dreaming. We're saying that once you understand your heart's desire that God planted within you, your dreams will parallel alongside your purpose of why God created you, turning out greater than you could have ever imagined!

B. What is your heart's desire?

C. How is this different than your dreams?

*

"Contentment. You've said that word over and over, Mr. and Mrs. Crager. It doesn't sound like a high goal. And joy isn't much better. I want to be excited and happy all the time, not content and joyful; those sound weak."

*

We understand, but happiness and excitement are only emotions, which we *guarantee* will go away with time; it always does. Be honest. You know this as fact in your own life. Why? Because as we change, our interests change. The world around us constantly changes. The situations in our lives change, and most of the time when things change, it's usually not what we expected, wanted, or planned. Plus, there are a plethora of other emotions fighting to come out of us sooner or later.

Joy comes from the heart and has its greatest impact on us when our world continues to change and let us down. Our relationship with God can always be the same yesterday, today, and tomorrow. God is the One that wants to fill our heart's desire, because He put it there in the first place. But first, we must begin to have a close relationship with Him to understand this supernatural gift and blessing.

In His supernatural ways, He can take all the things that we've explained about dreams and paint a true picture that will help guide us to have a successful and content life. He can also fulfill our fourth relational priority—our career—far beyond what we could imagine: one that *does not* need to be time exhausting, energy-sucking, emotionally and physically stressful, worrisome, and family destroying. We know this because, we have been there many times.

After saying all that, we are not forgetting about the stay-at-home moms and dads. That is a full-time career and a half, to say the least! Everything we have discussed is for you as well.

D. Are you content with your life and career? If not, why?

*

"Sounds too simple, not practical, and useless for where my career and family are at right now."

*

We understand, but at this moment, and most of the time, we are looking at our lives from a snail's ground perspective, only seeing things that are directly in front of us. Compared to an eagle eye viewpoint from high above, seeing the whole picture down below. We need to grasp the relationship with God, so He can free us from sluggishly crawling on the ground, and begin to soar.

We've come up with some analogies or similes we call "*secret powers*" that can affect not only our thinking, but perspective and direction for how we have the ability to *make wise choices* personally, for our careers and our family relationship. Slowly read the "*secret powers*" that everyone has within them:

- The power of having *nothing* is comparing an empty treasure box to a full trash can. We have the opportunity to start fresh, and fill our lives with what we want, or what God knows we need, instead of having to throw away other people's garbage. Only let God influence us, and not man's confused and messy understanding of what is going to fill our heart's desires.

- The power of *failure* is having hands-on experience and knowledge of what success is, and being able to understand its limits and our own, compared to a healthy young adult wearing a diaper. They are too scared, lazy, or full of excuses to sit on a toilet. This means that *if we are scared of failure, lazy, or full of excuses, we will never be successful or get anywhere in life.* We'll sit in our own poop the rest of our lives. We might as well hold on to dreams, because that's all our lives will be filled with, which leaves no room for the desires of our heart.

- The power of *flexibility* is like trying to bend a dry spaghetti noodle, compared to pulling back a compound bow to shoot arrows. With flexibility, we can move around filled with power, and be reshaped by God to fit different environments to be able to hit our targets. A dry spaghetti noodle will shatter into useless pieces the first time it's challenged, never moving forward or launching anything. Again, our heart's desire will never be filled.

- The power of a *vision* is comparing us wearing a blindfold, versus looking through binoculars. We will always be stagnant, or only move inches at a time blindfolded, never achieving a destination. Or, we could anticipate the terrain ahead by being inspired by God for a purpose to move forward towards a different and better future, which will fill our heart's desires.

- The power of *time* is like jumping off a cliff with or without a parachute. We could dive off and free fall without a parachute, only focusing on how hard or impossible it will be to avoid our demise, watching the ground coming at us at lighting speed. Or with a parachute, we would have the time to peer around and enjoy the sights, sounds, and smells around us that God created, as we softly glide through the sky, giving our body an exhilarating experience until we safely land at a target our heart was desiring.

- The power of *attitude* is comparing a piece of paper to a sponge when drench in water. We will disintegrate in the water as paper. Or, we could be indulged as a sponge, soaking up life and wisdom from God that our heart desires.

- The power of the *heart* is comparing us standing on soft sand versus a firm rock. Sooner or later, we will sink into the sand, being buried alive. Or, we could firmly be placed on a rock to live a life that fills our heart's desires.

- The power of *faith* goes beyond our reach and understanding. Without it, emptiness will *always* be our destiny, as our *worldly dreams only remain life's illusion of triumph.*

"My thoughts are nothing like your thoughts," says the Lord. "And my ways are far beyond anything you could imagine. For just as the heavens are higher than the earth, so my ways are higher than your ways and my thoughts higher than your thoughts."

Isaiah 55:8-9

E. Are you surprised about these "secret powers?" Which of them do you use?

F. Which ones are missing that could best impact your life?

I (D. L.), personally, have had many unique jobs when I was young, and have started and operated many businesses to success over the years. But success is a fragile word in the eye of the beholder, and is a delicate process, unless we press forward from the world's perspective.

The world tells us we must put in an excessive amount of time, excruciating hard work, go in debt by borrowing money, and sadly sacrifice much or all, if we're going to be successful. We can, at times, completely ignore who we may hurt, or what we might lose along the way, as long as we put one hundred percent of ourselves into achieving this success that we had dreamed of having one day.

Over twenty-five years ago with one of my businesses, I was there whole-heartedly believing this was the only way to successfully fill my dreams. I was working until the work was all done, or until I couldn't stay awake anymore. My attitude was, "I will be the best in everything I do, no matter what. I will never lose a customer and the phone and emails will always be answered until they stop ringing or coming in." Plus, I thought I had to work harder and longer hours to make more money. Especially because the bills were piling up, personally and in the business, even though I was making good money and the business was strong and profitable.

My insides were continually a mess, as my emotions and spiritual life bounced all over the place. I had little to no time for my life-long, cherished activities which I had actually put in their proper order some years earlier (I'll talk about that in the next chapter). But most of all, I *wasn't* spending time with my family, not to mention God.

Here's a fragment of the true story. For a long time, I would get home from work a little later than normal working hours, bringing my work home to make sure it all got done. My wife would call out to my office, "Dinner's ready," and my response would be, "I'll be there in a minute." After a while, she would call out, "your dinner is in the microwave," as my response would be the same, "I'll be there in a minute." Later she would call out, "I'm putting the kids to bed," and my response would be the same as my last, when she would say, "I'm going to bed." You can see just a glimpse of the nightmare by passing all the important evening events with my family, just so I could work more to be successful and make more money.

What an awful and wasteful time in our lives. I didn't like who I had become, or what I was doing. No longer was it a happy dream to have another business, as the career became a burdensome job, and my title of "President of the company" might as well have been "slave of the business."

From the world's perspective, I knew I had to sacrifice if I was going to be successful for me and my family, and ultimately reach my dreams. But the whole truth of what was happening was that I had allowed my life to get out of order, as my priorities were all over the place.

Then God spoke to me. I had consciously and subconsciously been crying out for help. Our money situation was bleak, even though work was very busy. My body was full of aches and pains, and I wasn't sleeping at night because I was constantly worrying. My body, mind, and heart were stressed out.

My kids and wife were doing things all the time without me, as the intimate times with my wife was...well, you figured out that pathetic picture.

God's words came to me late in the evening and were clear and simple. He said (paraphrasing), *"I want to you to stop working at five o'clock every day for thirty days. Stop answering the phone and worrying about losing customers if you don't answer when they call. Stop worrying about your bills and how much money you have in the bank. All I ask for is thirty days to prove to you that I am God and am your ultimate Provider. I need to demonstrate to you what truly is your heart's desire."*

It took everything I had in me, but I took a deep breath and walked away from the desk in my home for the last time. Every day I got home after working normal hours and spent every evening with my family.

This is when I truly began to know who my children were, as they got to know their father. As for my wife, well...you can fill in the blank!

Physically my body began to feel normal and healthy again. My emotions simmered down as my mind became clearer than it had been in a long time. But most of all, my spirit took off and began to soar! I was free! It was like I had burst out of the dark depths of the ocean, having held my breath the whole time, now being able to fill my lungs full of refreshing and rejuvenating air, giving me life once more.

It was about twenty days later when I checked on my personal and business accounts. Instantly, the blinding veil covering my heart and mind's eye were raised, and the extraordinary God of miracles came alive in *my* life. I instantly came to the realization that He does know me intimately. He knew how and when it was time to prove Himself to begin my transformation process of who I was as a follower of Jesus, a husband, father, and business owner. Before this, I had always known of Jesus and walked a religious life. But at that moment, and having *nothing* to do with the money, but how and why the money was in my accounts, transformed my knowledge and understanding of God. I have had a heart relationship with Him ever since.

Let me make one thing very clear. I *do not* treat my relationship with Jesus like He's Santa Claus. Nor do I buy into the theologies that because I'm a born-again Christian, and if I financially give enough, have enough faith, and pray enough, God will miraculously provide for what I want or dream of, and answer my prayers the way I want or think they should be answered. Nor do I think it will keep painful situations out of my life.

I do believe He will always provide for our needs, and be with me through everything, continually helping me to stay as close as I can to Him.

> Don't worry about anything; instead, pray about everything. Tell God what you need, and thank him for all he has done. Then you will experience God's peace, which exceeds anything we can understand. His peace will guard your hearts and minds as you live in Christ Jesus.
>
> Philippians 4:6-7

"And we know that God causes everything to work together for the good of those who love God and are called according to his purpose for them" (Romans 8:28).

His purpose for us is to love Him, serve Him, and to serve and love others to grow His Kingdom. It's not the other way around, which is the human dream: to be selfish and grow our own kingdom. God knows exactly what each of us needs in order to continually draw us closer to Him, to be more like Him, and eventually join Him in paradise. That is the good He is talking about. It's not saving us from the hurdles and situations, or stepping on porcupines or in mud puddles in our journey, which can be exhausting and painful. But He helps us successfully through and around them, because He is *with* us the whole time.

The gift of having a heart's desire aligns perfectly with who God is and what His purpose is for us, in all we do. That includes our careers!

G. What changes do you need to do in your career to finally begin to fulfil your heart's desire, and healthily grow your relationship with your family and God?

Chapter 8

Power Source

We are finally to number five, our activities relationship: hobbies, sports, video games, social media, watching television, working out, reading, ministry, entertainment, etc. This relationship is different than all the others. It's an *extra*, a *bonus* in life that *we get to do, not have to do*. We *do not* need this relationship to live and progress our life and our families.

*

"Then this isn't really a relationship, if you put it that way."

*

Okay, let us ask you some questions. Do these things cause our emotions to go up and down? Do we make time in our day or week for these things? Do we feel accomplishment and satisfaction when we do these things? Do we spend our hard-earned money on these things?

Of course, we do, just like we do for our children, spouse, and job. In that perspective, activities need to be categorized as one of the five of our relationships. So, how do we put these simple things out of order in our lives, when obviously our spouse, children, God, and having a job, are much more important? It doesn't take a rocket scientist to figure that out.

No, it doesn't, but we do it all the time, and for some, it's a blinding everyday *habit*.

We're not going to hash out the issues with this relationship that we've already covered in chapter three, when we were discussing what or who is our master, that contributes to negatively rearranging the priorities in our lives.

A. What do you and your spouse do that fits into this fifth relationship?

The next questions below are doozies, when we first ask this one perplexing question. Having our fifth relationship basically meant for hobbies, recreation, entertainment, relaxation, doing good works, etc., does it put the other four natural and necessary relationships in danger because we do it, or them so much?

- Does it put your family *at risk* of being *financially harmed*?
- Does it put your family *at risk* of having *minimal, to no time* spent together? The family basically gets your leftovers.
- Does it put your family *at risk* of having *your attention and responsibility stolen* from them?

- Does it put your family *at risk* of *not knowing* who their mother or father, husband or wife is?

- Does it put your family *at risk* of being *misdirected, mislead, led astray,* led to dead ends, however we want to put it, that *will lie or influence them to wrongly prioritize* their own relationships? This is especially for your children and their future.

Whether you know this or not, *we will be judged*, for the lives entrusted to us -our children- to provide, nurture, train and guide safely through life, if we put them at risk spiritually because we selfishly wanted to have *fun, be entertained, or even admired for our good deeds?* Jesus said, "But if you cause one of these little ones who trusts in me to fall into sin, it would be better for you to have a large millstone tied around your neck and be drowned in the depths of the sea" (Matthew 18:6).

We understand that we need to take a break to have fun and relax here and there, it's healthy. We understand that some activities inspire us in healthy ways. We understand that some activities bring the family closer together in a healthy manner. We understand we have gaps in the day with nothing to do at times, so we fill it with our extra activities.

We also understand that our activities can give us an *elusive purpose and a false identity* that will eventually control us to the point, it can destroy us, and all our relationships combined.

*

"Take it easy, it couldn't get that bad."

*

No? Then let me (D. L.) tell you another true story of mine. I grew up in the Rocky Mountains. So naturally, I fished, hunted, skied, backpacked, and climbed mountains all the time. Being up in the wilderness smoothly became—you could say—a religion of mine.

Also, growing up I played competitive soccer since I was eight years old, almost year-round, and all through high school. Out of high school, I got a scholarship and played in college. During college I had the opportunity to play in other countries for a summer.

Let's move ahead a few years after college and into my third year of marriage. I still continually did all of my outdoor activities with my lifelong buddies, as well as now playing amateur indoor soccer, again with my friends.

My important outdoor activities took up a majority of every weekend year-round. As did my important men's soccer games that were played a couple times during the weekdays in the evenings.

Adding to this schedule I worked two jobs to keep up with the bills. My wife and I had a house, two very young children, and of course, a dog. My wife was a stay-at-home mom at the time, because we decided it is was best for the kids to have their parents raise them, instead of a babysitter, so she gave up her career for twelve years. Oh, not to forget, we attended the church I grew up in.

Now you have an eagle eye view I mentioned in a previous chapter. What picture do you see that I have painted for what our family life was like? To me, at my ground level snails view, it was a complete package. I had it all!

The *lens* that I was looking through, you know the one, me, myself and I, the identity of who I was—a great outdoors man, a successful athlete—consciously and subconsciously took precedence over how I made my life's decisions and arranged my family's daily schedules. This was all because *I* was not going to miss out on what I thought life was all about—*having fun*!

Everything was running smoothly, just the way I envisioned and planned my life to be. It never hit me how bad it was, or more importantly, how bad *I was* at being a father, husband, and leader of the family, until one weeknight around 9 p.m., when one of my buddies picked me up to go play a soccer game on the other side of town.

Shelly was very tired that evening. Besides watching our two children, she also babysat two other kids every day of the week, all day. To add to her busy day, she had not been feeling well. Just before my friend got to our house, Shelly started throwing up. Being the good father and husband I thought I was, I took our kids to safely play in another room, as I attended to my wife any way I could, then the doorbell rang...

Sorry, I had to pause. I get so emotional every time I get to this part of the story.

The doorbell rang and instantly, as though a light switch was flipped, everything that I was responsible for, my children and sick wife, just vanished. *My true identity,* the relationship that was number one in my life, took over. I had conditioned myself emotionally, mentally, physically, and spiritually that I was doing the right thing, and left my family to conquer what gave their family leader—me— his identity. I had put all the other relationships in their twisted order down the line somewhere.

I told Shelly, still leaning over the toilet, that the kids were in the other room playing, and asked her if there was anything else I could get for her before I left. She looked at me with the most helpless and hurtful expression and said, "No, go play." And so, I left.

*

"You jerk!"

*

No, worse than that. I was worthless human garbage, lower than low!

That is when Jesus had to step in. As soon as I got into my friend's car, I began to feel strange. I thought I may be getting sick because my wife was throwing up, and for a second, I blamed her.

Then my mind wouldn't let go for the rest of the evening, and days to come, seeing Shelly's painful expression and saying over and over, "go play."

To make a long story short, my mind, body, and spirit was in turmoil for a while, as Jesus was helping me with my first transformation of responsibilities and priorities in my young adult life, through situations and the influence of different people. It was a fight at first. A fight for my life, or was it *fear* of losing my identity? Either way, I assume it felt similar to when someone has an addiction to a *controlling* substance.

Yes, I did just say that! To go back to what I talked about earlier, my activities had become my *master*!

In the chain of supernatural events, one specific couple, older than my wife and I from church, invited us over for dinner one night. Over time, as our relationship and *their influence* in our lives grew stronger and stronger, both Shelly and I were gently being guided towards a healthy family lifestyle, which later turned into what we now call *a life in order*.

As I look back to those early years, it became clear once the dust settled, how I got to the hopeless grave I did.

- It *was not* because I was very good at the activities.

- It *was not* because I had a great time doing the activities.

- It *was not* that I thought I had to have the activities.

I figured it out following the trail back to when it all started. I was *told, taught, influenced, and given the example thereof,* by my father since I was a young child, that activities/having fun—whatever it is for you—is what life was *all* about.

- We work hard to have fun.

- We work so we can afford to have fun.

- We schedule our lives (evenings, weekends, vacations, etc.) to have fun.

- Basically, work and everything else in life is used as the catapult to propel us to the goal of having fun, which is an *illusion of eternal glory and happiness!*

I need to interject here. My father loved his children and his wife. He was one of the hardest working and giving men I ever knew. He was a man that knelt every night at his bed to pray. Overall, he was a responsible man, no question.

But as children, what we saw, heard, and experienced our father value the most in life, always drew our attention to the activities which was the fountain of happiness to him. Not healthy relationships with his family or even God.

By now, if you haven't figured it out, happiness is always fleeting, because it's only temporary, and ultimately just a false dream that is always chased and never caught.

By the way, my story above didn't start with my dad. He desperately grasped ahold of having fun—his activities—for dear life, because his father did not allow him to play or have *any* fun all through his childhood. In the eyes of his whole family, my grandfather's focus— first priority—in life was working, sun up to sun down, six days a week, while God came in a close second by shoveling and stomping God down his son's—my fathers—throat. So much so, that God became a religion to my father, and his relationship with God was confusing and a hard one for him to understand. True story.

Are you seeing clearly that what we prioritize and value in life will have a negative or positive chain reaction effect on our children and grandchildren? Pause here for a moment and think about your upbringing.

B. What is your story?

C. Can you think of ways that can positively influence the generations below you if you put your own relationships in order right now?

Moms and dads, what are we demonstrating and teaching our children to value so that they have a *life in order*? It's our responsibility, as we have the opportunity to change and positively influence the destiny of our generations to come, even if it's by one percent. It starts with us!

The moral of this book is that *God must always be our first relational priority, so the rest of our relationships can grow and thrive.* God will persistently and lovingly, in any way He can—as He has done for us many times—keep drawing us to Him.

God is love, and when that love becomes the core of our hearts, joy will then be able to continuously flow through our veins, and will be the satisfying *contentment* for our mind, body, and spirit through all hurdles and circumstances as *hope leads the way*!

Look at the cover of this book again with the vending machine out of order. The different relationships, items, hurdles or situations *within* the machine, *are not* the problem. Why, because the machine—what gives us true life—is *not* plugged in.

It's out of order because the power *source—humanity's power source, Jesus Christ—is not part of our daily lives*. When and why did we unplug our power source—God—out of our lives? Or has our machine (life) always been out of order, because we never plugged Him in, in the first place?

We are already born broken, needing to be reborn through Jesus Christ, as Satan relentlessly pursues us to focus on everything else in our lives, except for our true power source and Savior, Jesus Christ!

So, what do you need to do now? Take the first step, and plug God into your life. In prayer, acknowledge to Jesus that you are broken and have sinned against Him (like us and everyone else), and that you want Him in your life to be your Lord and Savior. Ask Him to fill you with the Holy Spirit, and then surrender your whole life to Him. It's that simple. Once you're finally *alive with the Spirit of*

God—the Holy Spirit—you will begin the extraordinary journey that will fill your heart's desires.

The Visual to Remember

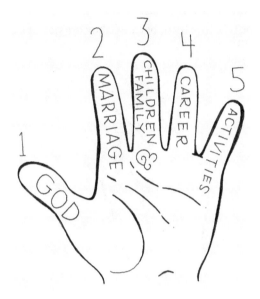

Why the hand? Very simple! With God in the thumb position, He will always be special, and pointing in a different direction than His creations tend to go. Being in an imperfect world, we will always drift away, whether we mean to or not. Remember what Isaiah 55:8-9 taught us.

When God is number one in our lives, and we have a healthy relationship with Him, the second relationship—marriage—has the greatest chance of being healthy.

With our marriage in the number two position, having the opportunity to be healthy because of God being our number one relationship, our children in the number three position will have the greatest opportunity to have a healthy marriage of their own in the future, because their parents demonstrated it, by living a life in order. It's a natural flow.

You can piece together the fourth and fifth priorities by now.

If we have all of our relationships in a different order than we have been explaining, God has a hard time—not impossible—touching all the different relationships, because they are out of order.

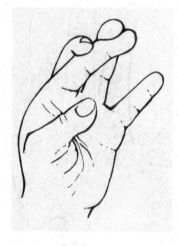

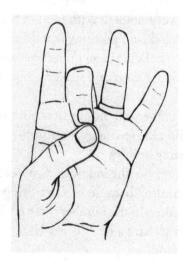

When our relationships are in order, God can easily touch each relationship one at a time. Also, when our relationships are in order, it's natural and easier for God to touch *all* our relationships at once, bringing that balance, joy, and contentment into our lives.

He knows what His children need for hope to thrive in a broken world. Put your life in order, and live in great expectations of what our extraordinary God will do, not only for you, but for your spouse and children as well. Jesus will *not* let you down, but instead He will lift you up to new heights you never thought were possible. We are living proof that we have a great and mighty God who truly and faithfully loves us!

We have focused this book on relationships. Why? Because everything in this world from start to finish is *Simply Relational*.

About the Authors

D. L. and Shelly Crager are a dynamic and fun couple that are experienced, insightful, and informative when it comes to relationships.

Shelly has been in the teaching field in administration with Christian schools for over twenty years and is currently completing her doctorate.

D. L. has owned many successful businesses as well as been extremely instrumental in church leadership. He has written several other Christian books, with many more on the way.

Besides a plethora of professional experience, they personally have developed decades of wisdom as Christian parents and grandparents. Along with personal achievements, life's hurdles and difficult situations have matured, enriched, and strengthened them to be who they are today.

Their exciting and entertaining way of writing stories will keep readers captivated. But most of all, the wisdom they have to share will encourage everyone to have great expectations of our extraordinary God and to live a life full of hope.

Additional Resources
for

"Is Your Life Out of Order?"
a Study Guide and Video Teaching
can be found at

www.dlcrager.com

Also, check out other books written by
D. L. Crager